The fridge

Mike Wheeler and Davic

Fridge is short for "refrigerator". This book is about when fridges were first made and the way modern fridges work. To explain all this, the book introduces some scientific facts about heat and insulation.

If you are using the book to find out particular facts about fridges, you do not have to read it all. Look in the **contents** (below) or the **index** (at the back) to find the best pages to help you. Then just read as much as you need to read.

The basic facts are given in big print, and more detailed information is in smaller print.

Contents

1 What is a fridge?

A fridge is a cold box that stays cold. The box can be small like the one in your kitchen, or it can be very big. In some factories, they are so big that you can walk around inside them. Fridges are the modern way of keeping food cold.

Some fridges have a freezer included.

Some people work all day in factory fridges.

The fridge in your home is quite small. Shops have larger fridges that can hold lots of frozen foods. Butchers have fridges as big as a room. They keep their meat hanging from the ceiling.

Factories that have to store a lot of food have whole buildings that are fridges. The people who work in these buildings have to wear special clothes and gloves to protect them from the cold.

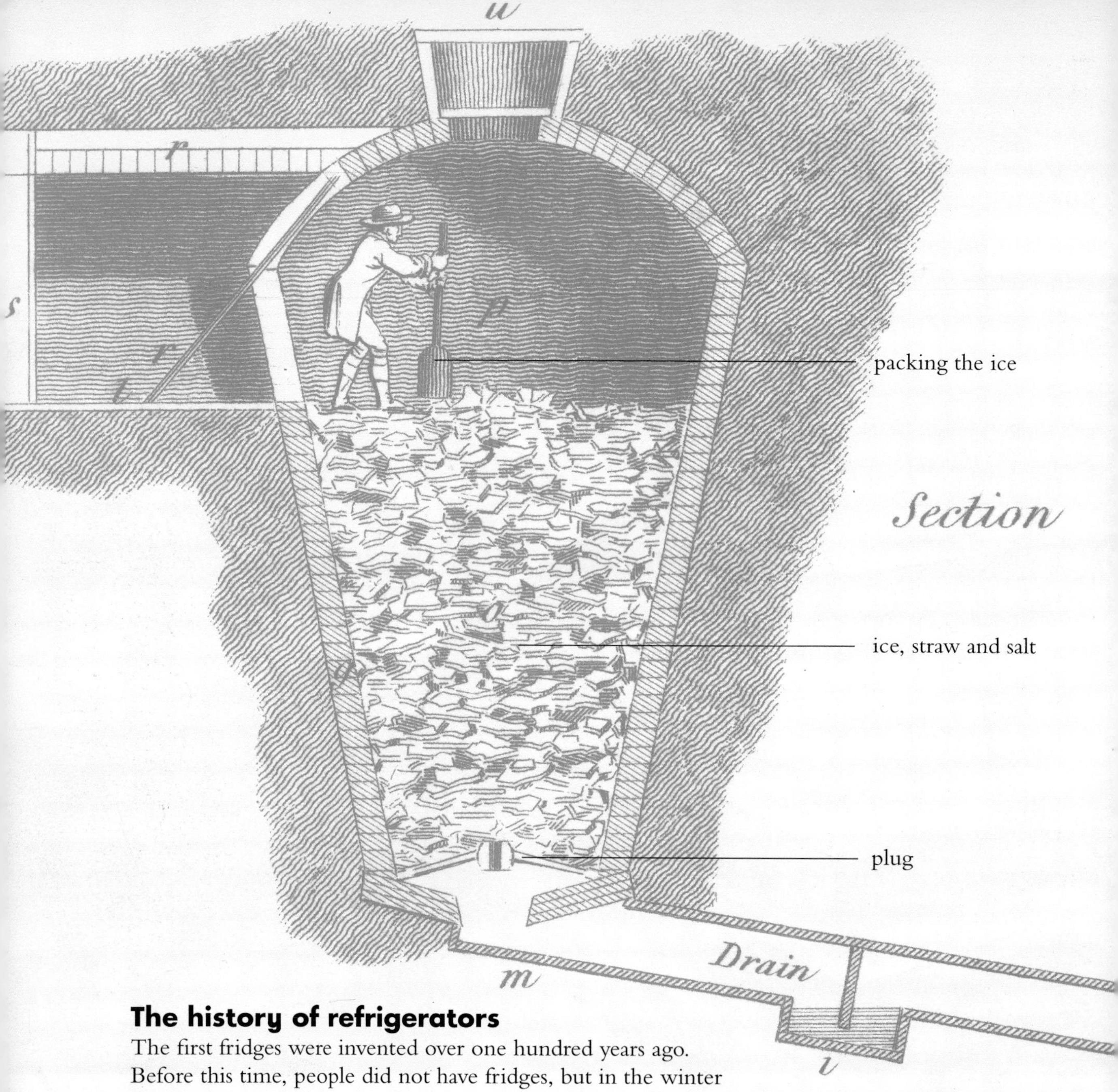

The history of refrigerators

The first fridges were invented over one hundred years ago. Before this time, people did not have fridges, but in the winter they had ice and snow.

They collected the ice from frozen lakes. They then wrapped it in straw and salted it to make it colder. The ice and food stayed frozen for most of the year. Some people had special rooms called ice houses. They put food and ice into the rooms.

Many homes were too small to have ice houses so they used a special container called an ice box. They filled part of the container with ice and the rest with food. Ice houses and ice boxes were used for many hundreds of years.

In 1834, a man called Jacob Perkins built a machine to make ice artificially. The first fridges were based on this machine. By 1870 some people already had fridges, but they were big and expensive so most people still used ice blocks to keep their food cold.

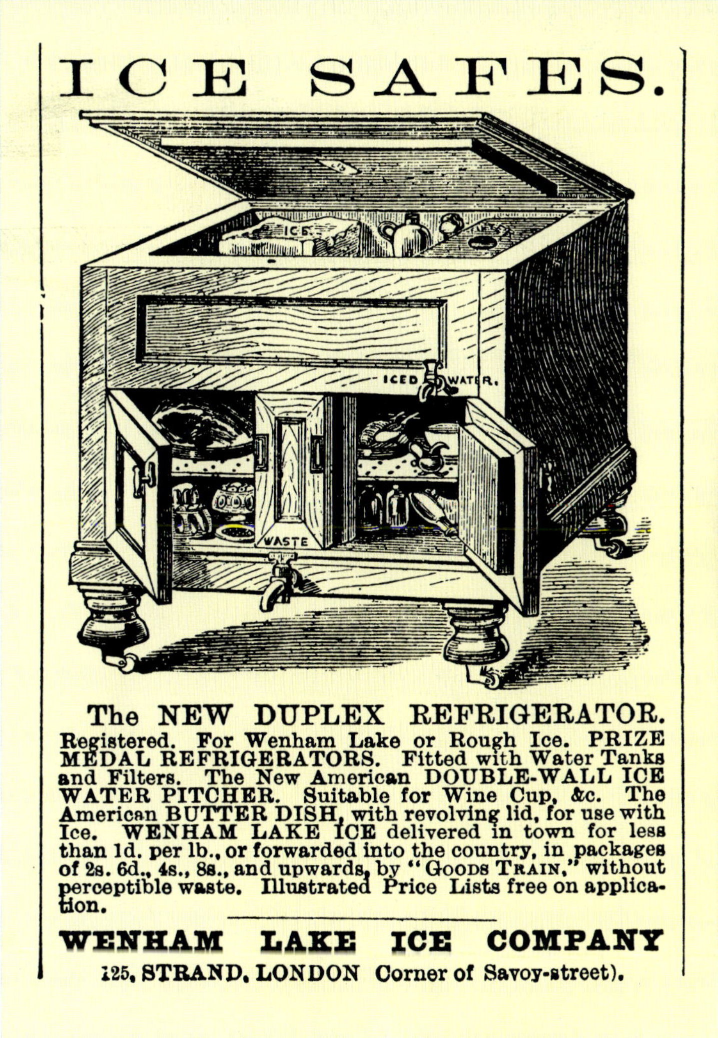

It was in the 1890s that more people realised that fridges were a good idea.

It was the weather in 1890 and 1891 that made people look at new ways of making ice. For instance, in 1890 in Sweden, there was a very mild winter, so there was very little snow and ice available.

In 1891 in America there was a very hot summer. At times like this, people realised that they needed reliable and cheap fridges to keep food fresh.

Modern refrigerators were first made and used in large numbers in the 1920s. This is also when the first frozen foods were sold.

2 How does a fridge work?

A fridge is a cold box. It is kept cold by a machine. The machine has many pipes, both inside and outside the box. The pipes take heat out of the box so that the box stays cold.

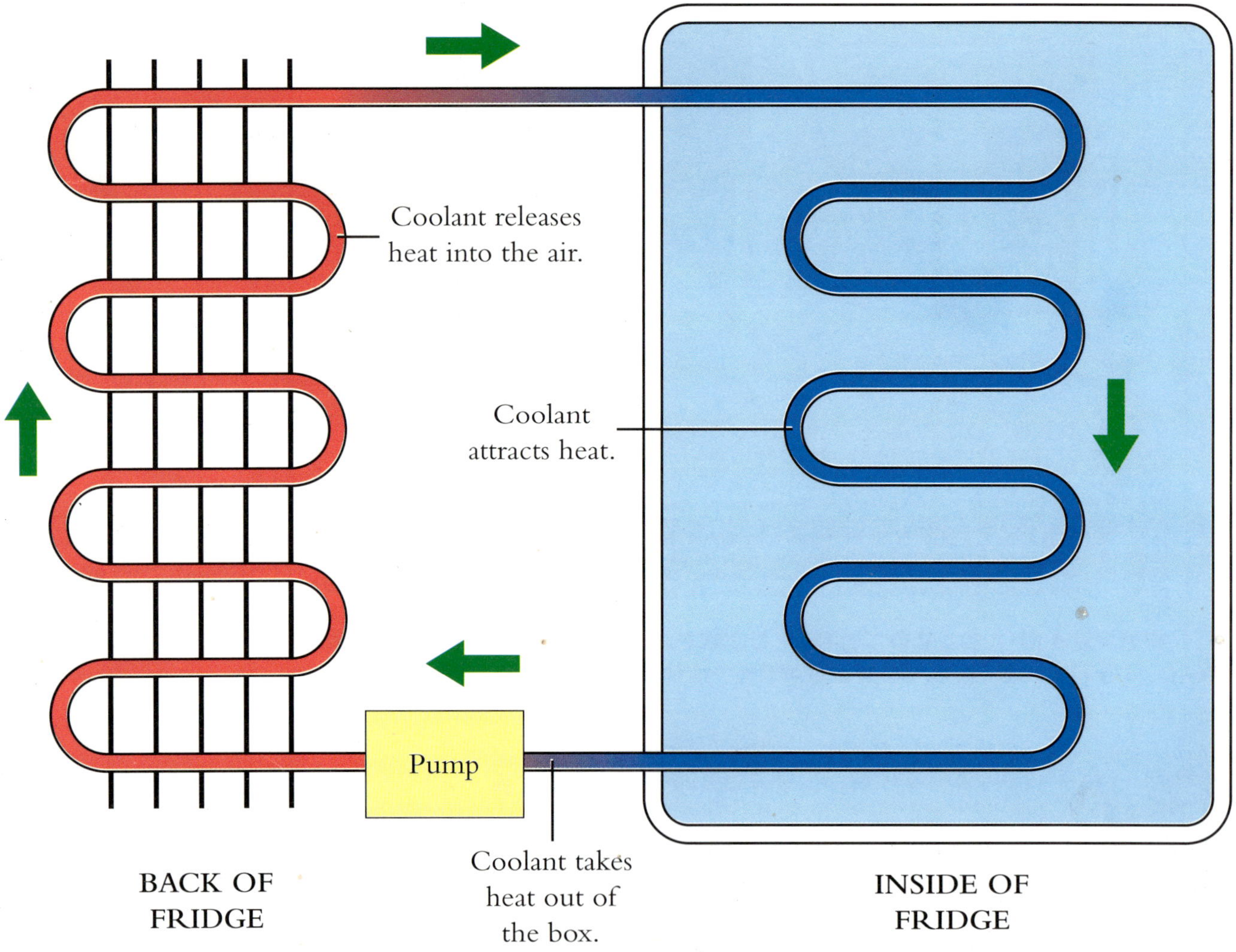

A diagram of how a fridge works.

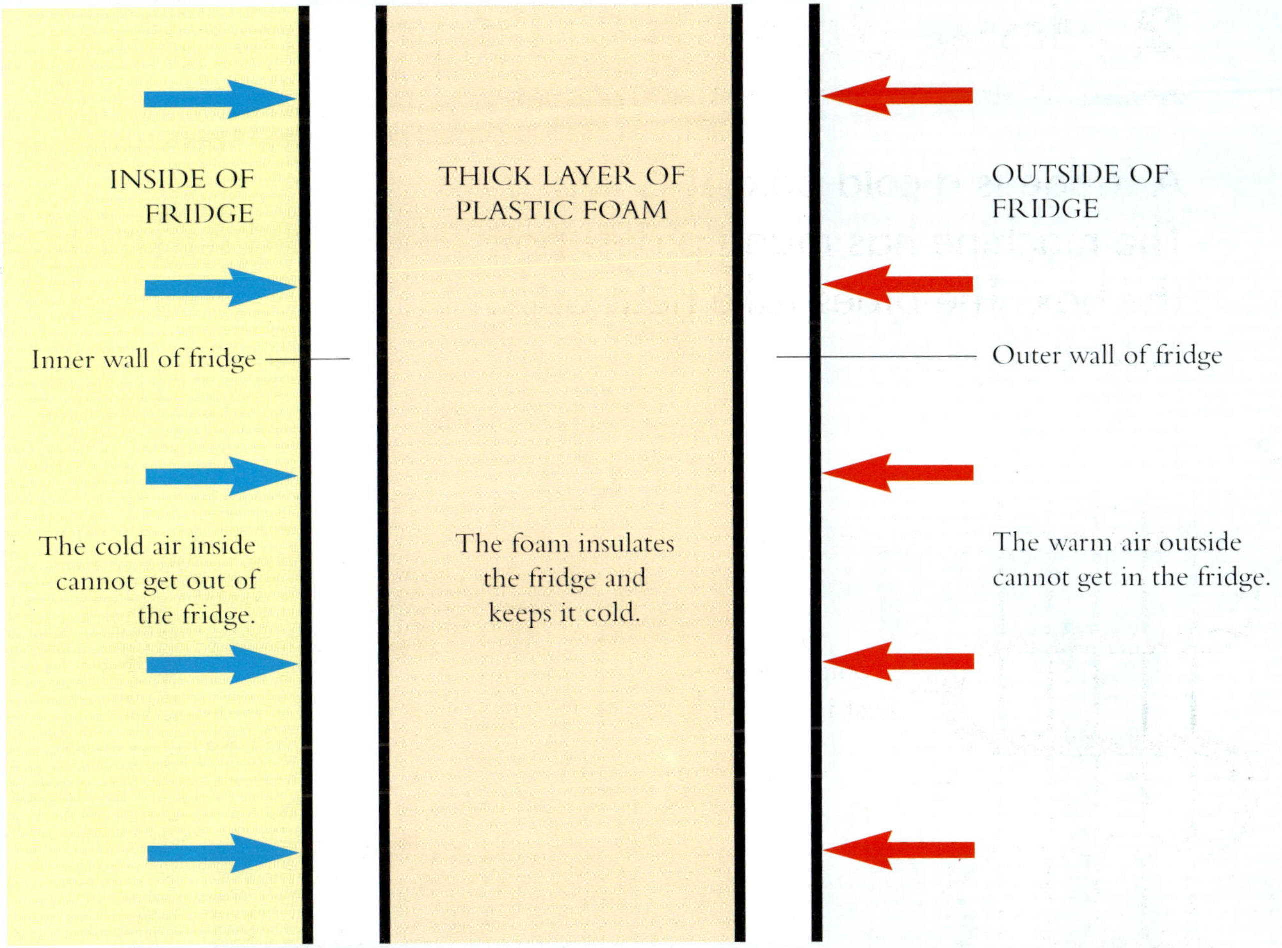

A diagram showing how a fridge is insulated.

A fridge is like a box, containing a machine which takes the heat away. This machine consists of

- a pump
- sealed pipes, inside and outside the fridge box
- a liquid (called coolant) inside the sealed pipes.

The pump pushes the liquid coolant through the pipes inside the fridge. As it goes, the coolant attracts heat out of the contents of the fridge and into itself. It takes this heat to the pipes outside the fridge, where it is released into the air.

There is also a thick layer of plastic foam around the refrigerator box. This insulates the box so that warmer air from outside cannot get inside.

Parts of a fridge

The pump in a fridge is called a compressor. It pumps liquid coolant through a set of pipes that run inside and outside the refrigerator. The pipes on the outside look like a black radiator.

The coolant collects the heat energy from inside the fridge and carries it to the set of black pipes on the outside of the fridge. Here the heat energy escapes into the air.

The inside of a fridge is made of hard smooth materials, like plastic, glass and stainless steel. Some parts are made of metal covered in plastic. These materials do not have sharp corners, so they can be easily cleaned.

The door is insulated. It has a tight seal round the edge so that heat cannot leak in. Most doors are kept tightly shut by magnets (see page 20).

The cooling pipes behind a fridge.

Taking the CFCs safely out of an old fridge.

Fridges and the environment

The liquid coolant in old fridges can harm the environment. It is called freon, and it is a CFC. CFCs have helped to make holes appear in the ozone-layer.

CFCs were also used in making the plastic foam insulator around old fridges, so old fridges were not "ozone-friendly". Scientists today have replaced these dangerous materials with new ones that are not so dangerous.

If you need to get rid of an old fridge you should contact your local council. They will safely get rid of the CFCs which are inside the fridge.

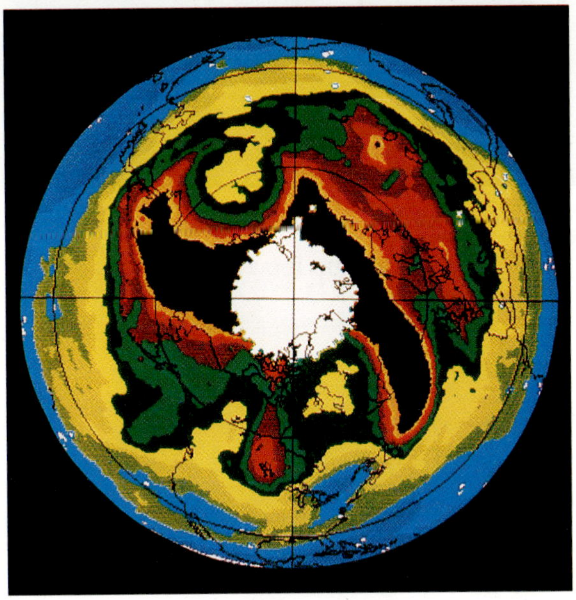

The white patch is a hole in the earth's ozone layer, thought to be caused by CFCs.

3 Keeping food cold

You can store fresh food in a fridge or a freezer. Both machines keep food cold. If food is kept cold, it stays fresh (and safe to eat) for longer. A freezer can keep food safe to eat for many months.

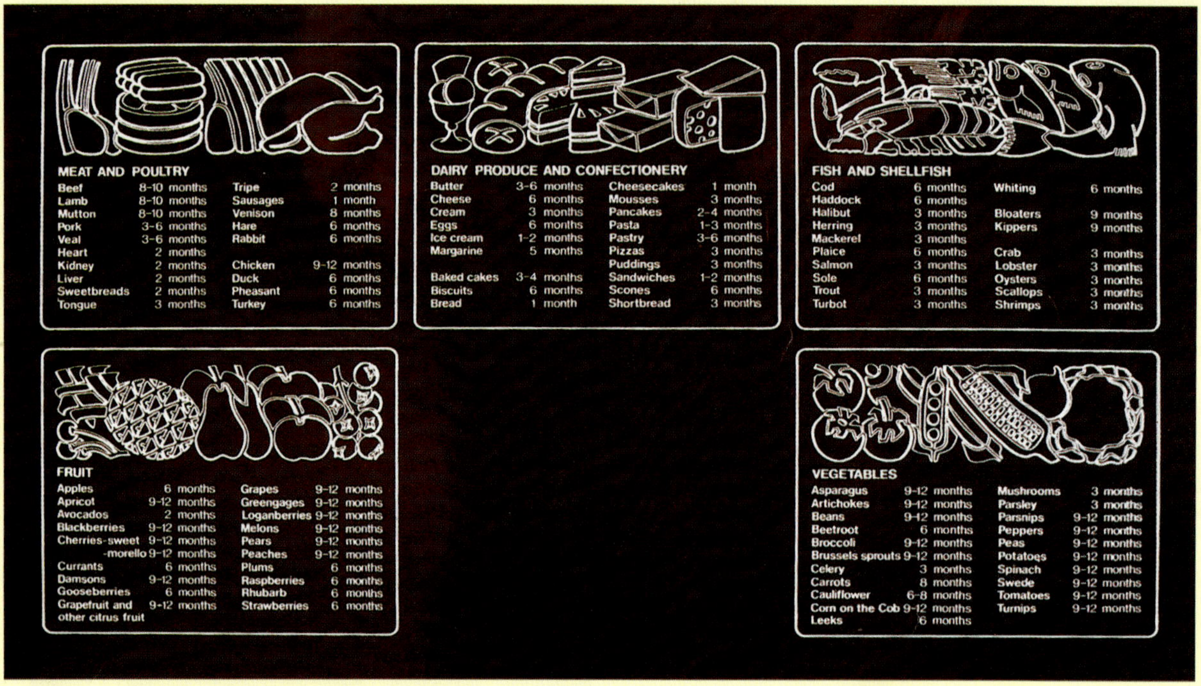

↑ The food is star rated. The more stars the longer the food keeps.

Freezer star ratings. →

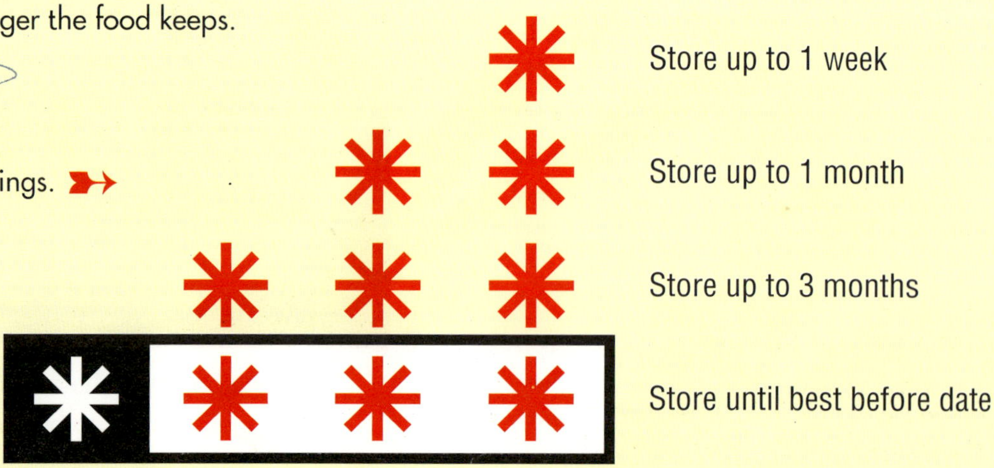

A fridge must be set to a temperature of 5°C or below. This low temperature slows down the growth of the micro-organisms which make food go bad.

A fridge thermometer is an important instrument in the kitchen. You can place it inside the fridge and check it to make sure that the temperature is 5°C or below.

A fridge thermometer tells you the temperature.

A freezer is much colder than a refrigerator. It is so cold that it can freeze food hard. Some foods can be stored for up to a year in a freezer. When food is taken out of the freezer you must warm it up before cooking it. This is called defrosting.

Once food has been defrosted, it must be eaten quickly because it will not keep for long.

Most foods can be frozen in a freezer, but some are destroyed by the intense cold.

Storing and transporting food

When food has to travel a long way, it is often stored in large fridges or freezers. Frozen meat is transported in specially-designed ships to ports and harbours. Special freezer lorries then take the meat to shops or supermarkets to be sold, or to large warehouses where it is stored. When the meat is stored for a long time, it must have a very low temperature – at least minus 18°C.

Fish on trawlers are packed in ice.

Some food, such as fruit and vegetables, can be stored and transported using a technique called gas storage. This means that food is chilled and then oxygen is removed from it. The oxygen is then replaced with carbon dioxide. When this has been done, micro-organisms will not grow as easily on the food, so it will stay fresh.

The food is stored in a chilled part of the ship.

An American food scientist called Clarence Birdseye first discovered how to freeze food. This was in 1928. Since then, his name has become very well-known.

Clarence Birdseye.

Activity

Collect a selection of fresh fruits and salad foods. Prepare a sample of each in a container or in a bag. Leave each in the freezer overnight. Remove them and let each defrost. What are suitable for freezing?

Strawberries lose their shape if they are frozen.

4 Keeping food fresh

All fresh food can go bad. If you eat bad food, it can make you ill. Food goes bad more quickly in warm places. A fridge helps to keep food fresh for a few days longer.

Mould grows easily on fruit.

Damp, warm food can easily go bad.

Food goes bad because the air is full of micro-organisms. If a micro-organism lands on food, it can begin to grow. Micro-organisms can only be seen under a microscope. They are living things that like damp, warm food. As they grow, they can make poison. The poison can make you very ill if you eat it. This illness is called food poisoning.

To keep food as fresh as possible, it must be protected from micro-organisms. Food that is carefully wrapped and placed in a cold place will last longer.

A fridge keeps food for a few days, but a freezer can make food last for up to a year. The freezer is so cold that the organisms will grow only very slowly.

There are instructions on the packets of many foods, telling you how long to store it.

Bacteria and other micro-organisms

Foods that can go bad easily are called perishable foods. They are moist and more likely to be spoiled by micro-organisms than other foods. There are three common types of micro-organisms known as yeasts, moulds, and bacteria. They can be found almost anywhere, especially in dust and furniture and even on your hands!

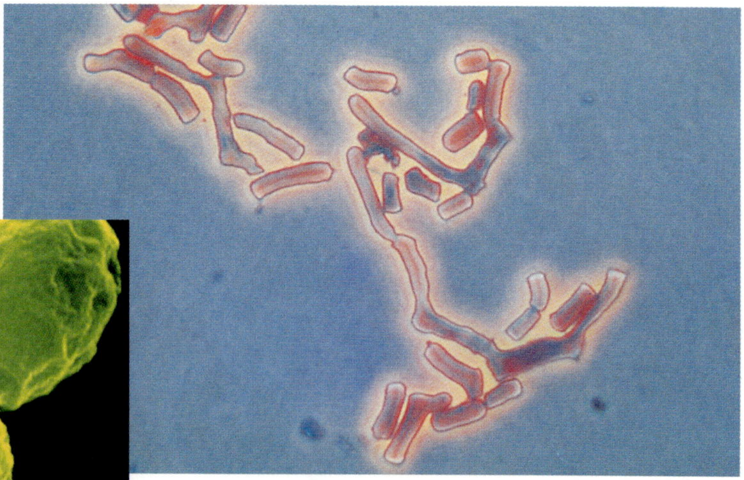

Mould magnified 120 times.

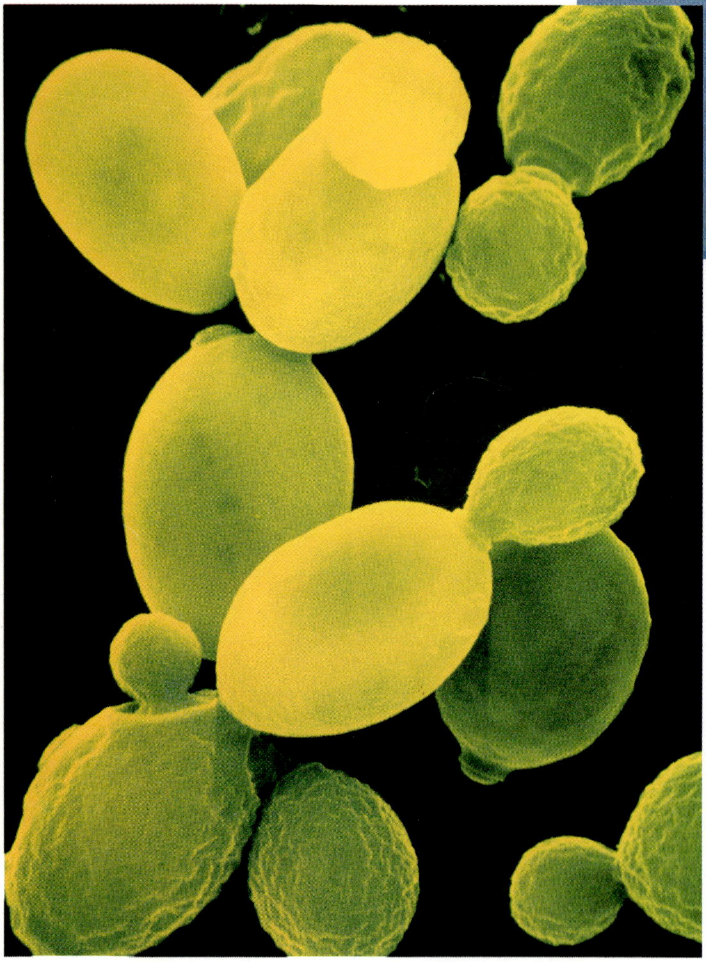

Yeast magnified 2,420 times.

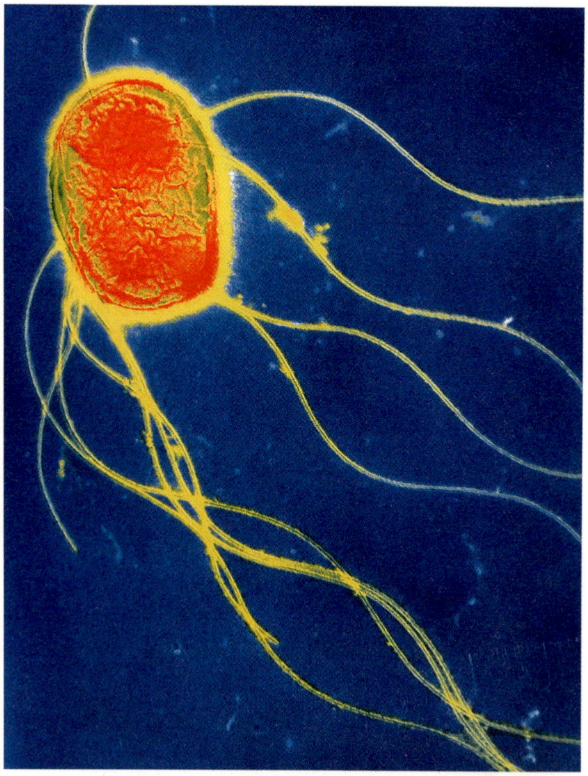

Bacteria magnified 13,100 times.

All fresh foods have dates on them to help the shopper.

How to protect food from bacteria

The most dangerous type of micro-organisms are bacteria. Bacteria are incredibly small forms of plant life. They grow by feeding on their environment. They grow particularly well on meat, especially pork and chicken.

When we store food, we have to protect it from bacteria. There are four important ways of preserving food. Each method involves removing one or more of the conditions needed for bacteria to grow.

The four methods for preserving food:

1 Removing moisture.
- We can dry foods to remove the moisture on which the bacteria can grow (for example, drying grapes so they become raisins).

2 Removing air.
- Bacteria are carried in the air. We can seal foods very tightly in cans or bottles so air cannot get to them.

3 *Spoiling* the food.
- We can pickle food in sugar or vinegar so that it lasts longer.

4 Controlling the temperature.
- We can keep food cold in a fridge or freezer so that it takes longer for bacteria to grow.
- We can make food very hot (for instance, boiling or microwaving) which kills off some bacteria.

Activity

Look at the packaging on supermarket shelves. Compare the *sell by* dates on frozen foods with those on fresh food. Look, for example, on the fish or meat counters. The frozen food will remain fit to eat for much longer.

We can never completely remove the bacteria. Some will always remain, so you should eat food promptly while it is still fresh.

5 Controlling your fridge

A fridge works by electricity. It has two special switches inside. One switch controls how cold the fridge gets. This is called a thermostat. The other switch turns the light on when you open the door. It also turns it off again when you close it.

This switch controls the temperature

Inside the fridge there is a simple push switch that turns the light on and off. It works in the same way as the switch that turns the light on and off when you open a car door.

As the door opens, it releases the switch. This makes a continuous circuit and turns the light on. As the door closes, it pushes onto the switch, breaking the circuit and turning the light off.

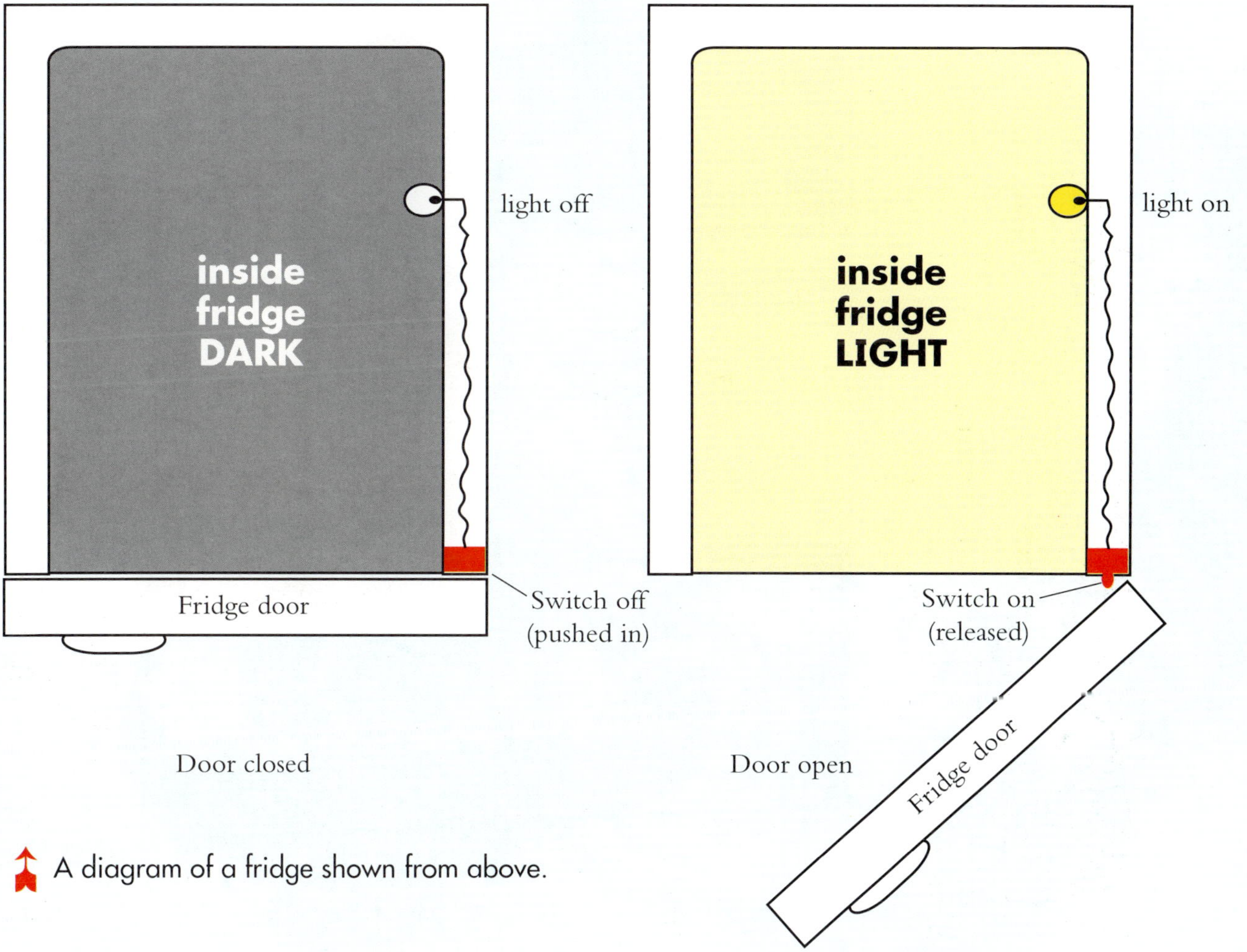

A diagram of a fridge shown from above.

The thermostat works in a different way to the light. As the temperature inside the fridge rises, it turns the cooler unit on. As the temperature falls below a set level it turns the cooling unit off.

Other parts of the fridge

Magnets

Magnets hold the door of a fridge shut. These magnets are hidden. A magnet will attract iron, steel or another magnet, so the frame of the door must have one of these things in it. The pulling action of the magnet only has an effect when the door is nearly closed.

The thermostat

The temperature inside a fridge is controlled by a special switch called a thermostat. The thermostat can be adjusted to keep the temperature inside the fridge cool, cold, or very cold.

The thermostat makes sure that the fridge is always cold even in very hot weather. In a heatwave, the cooler unit just has to work harder to overcome the heat. A freezer also has a thermostat to control it.

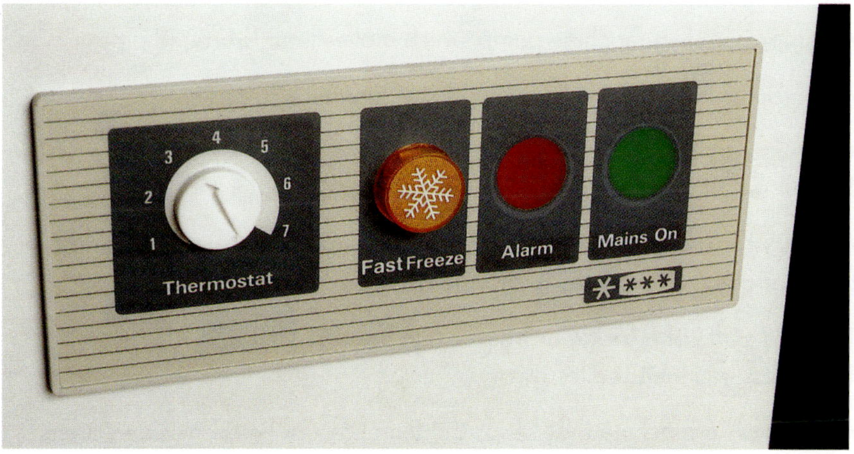

The thermostat unit of a freezer.

You can find thermostats in many machines that need to control temperature. In lots of houses, central heating and hot water for taps are controlled by thermostats.

Thermistors

Some large modern fridges do not use thermostats. They use thermistors instead. These are linked to a computer. The computer is then used to control the temperature, switching the cooler unit on and off as the temperature rises and falls.

Industrial freezers are controlled in this way. Thermistors are more accurate than thermostats and use much less energy.

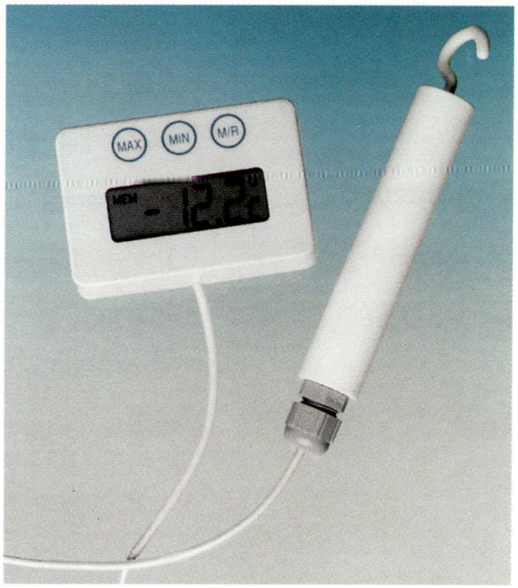

A thermistor from an industrial freezer.

Glossary

Bacteria — Bacteria are tiny living things that can only be seen through a microscope. Some bacteria can make you ill if you eat them. Bacteria can make food go bad.

CFC — CFC is a chemical used in many fridges to keep them cool.

Compressor — A compressor is a machine pump which moves liquids around pipes.

Container — A container is anything like a box or jar, in which things can be kept.

Continuous circuit — A continuous circuit is made when electric wires are joined together. This allows the electricity to flow through them.

Coolant — A coolant is a liquid which stops machines getting too hot. The liquid carries the heat away and passes it into the air around the machine.

Defrost — The cold parts of a fridge or freezer can become iced up. To defrost you melt the ice away.

Freezer — A freezer is a machine that keeps the temperature below freezing point. It can be used to store food.

Insulator — An insulator is something that doesn't allow heat to pass through it easily. It can keep hot things hot and cold things cold.

Micro-organism — A micro-organism is a tiny living creature that cannot be seen with the eye. A microscope is needed to see it.

Sensor — A sensor is something which tells a fridge if it is getting too cold or hot.

Ozone layer — The ozone layer is part of the atmosphere around the Earth. It is made up of gases which stop dangerous rays from the sun harming living things.

Temperature — Temperature is a measure of how hot something is.

Thermistor — A thermistor is often used to help to keep fridges at the correct temperature.

Thermostat — A thermostat is a small machine that keeps the temperature at the same level and so stops things getting too hot or too cold.

Yeast — Yeast is a tiny plant. Yeast is used to make bread. It is also used to make wine and beer.

Further Information

Books

101 Questions – How things Work, Dorling Kindersley.

Children's Illustrated Encyclopaedia, Dorling Kindersley.

Machines and How They Work, Dorling Kindersley.

The Kingfisher Book of How Things Work by Steve Parker, Kingfisher.

Index